STOLEN DREAM

Hugo D. Menendez

Library of Congress Control Number:		2018901166
ISBN:	Hardcover	978-1-5434-8003-0
	Softcover	978-1-5434-8004-7
	eBook	978-1-5434-8005-4

Print information available on the last page.

Edited by Elizabeth Mayhew Weeks
Cover design by Hugo D. Menendez.

Rev. date: 01/29/2018

To order additional copies of this book, contact:
Xlibris
1-888-795-4274
www.Xlibris.com
Orders@Xlibris.com
772302

Acknowledgements

On January 22, 1987, during the first session of the 100th congress, SENATOR LAWTON CHILES read into the congressional record the professional career of Mr. Menendez. His statement reads in part . . . "Hugo organized a highly trained team of accountants and investigators who uncovered extortion, union management payoffs, theft from union funds and pension and benefit plan funds and pension and benefit plan rip-offs. His leadership and guidance led to convictions in numerous racketeering cases involving the highest ranking labor racketeers in the country . . . . In 1984 through 1986 he received the ultimate accolade from his Nation by virtue of a Presidential appointment to the President's Commission on Organized Crime."

DEDICATION

This book, was written as a result of my wife Cleo's encouragement that I write a book about my many varied experiences while working for the Federal Government as well as my experiences as Secretary of Labor for the State of Florida and as a licensed private investigator.

When we were but mere children, she saw in me a potential that I was not aware of. If it had not been for her encouragement to be all I could be and her support, often times sacrificing her own potential, my career would have probably been that of a stock clerk at a local super market. She is my hero and was always the wind beneath my wings.

I thank Cleo for her encouragement and faith in me. My deepest regret is that she is not here to read the books that I have written as a result of her love, encouragement and faith in me.

ABOUT THE AUTHOR

Mr. Menendez began his government career conducting national security investigations. He also conducted some of the first background investigations of astronauts, most of whom, ultimately travelled to the moon. He enforced the Voting Rights laws in the 1960's and 70's all over the southern United States He was later employed by the U.S. Department of Labor's Labor Management Services Administration as supervisory special agent. He enforced the provisions of the Taft Hartley Act. Mr. Menendez later transferred to the U.S. Department of Justice's Miami Organized Crime Strike Force. He became the special agent in charge of the Office for Organized Crime and Labor Racketeering Section. Special Agent Menendez was appointed to President Reagan's Commission On Organized Crime, as staff investigator from 1984 to 1987. He served as secretary of labor for the State of Florida from 1987 to1992. Mr. Menendez participated in a joint venture with the law firm of Holland and Knight, a national law firm, after his retirement as Secretary of Labor. The company Corporate Integrity Services provided investigative services to the law fi rm. Mr. Menendez was Vice President and Senior Investigative Consultant of the company. Upon his retirement, from federal service, his government service history was read into the Congressional record by Senator Lawton Chiles during the first session of the 100th Congress. Eugene F.

Methvin, senior editor of Reader's Digest, wrote an article on Mr. Menendez and his contributions towards organized crime and labor racketeering Investigations in the August 1987 edition titled "Union in Bondage." Mr. Menendez at times was a visiting lecturer at the FBI Academy located In Quantico, Virginia. The lectures were on methods of conducting organized crime And labor racketeering investigations.

Mr. Menendez is a Korean War Veteran.

STOLEN DREAM

CHAPTER 1

Special Agent Menendez arrived at his office in Santurce, Puerto Rico at 8 a.m. He wanted to get an early start since he had to travel to Roosevelt Roads, the U. S. Naval Base on the eastern part of Puerto Rico. He was conducting an investigation for the Atomic Energy Commission dealing with nuclear submarines. His office was located on the second floor of the Publico Super Market which is located across the street from the Banco Popular. It had no address since in the San Juan metropolitan area utilizes a different system of addresses. When the old city of San Juan was populated dating back to the early 1600s the city was, and still is, a small area centrally located on the north coast of the island. Just as other towns of the era, San Juan has very narrow streets and the buildings are connected by common walls. It is a hindrance to utilize an automobile in the city. It is small enough that one can walk to any destination within the city. One of the major streets, if you can call it that, is Fortaleza Street. At the north end of the street is where the Governor's mansion is located, which is called the Fortaleza. Ponce De Leon occupied this building when he was the Governor of Puerto Rico. As San Juan began to develop suburbs, in the 20's a bus system was initiated. The buses left Old San Juan towards the outskirts of the city. The location where the bus made its first stop was called parada numero uno or stop number one. As the city grew, there were more stops added till this day when the stops number in the 50's or more. Special Agents Menendez's office was in the Parada number twelve. Utilizing the system of Paradas, when you get off at your stop, you look for the building where you need to go. When Special Agent Menendez first began working in Puerto Rico, he felt that it was a very stupid system. However as he became used to the system, he found it to be very workable.

Because of the time zone, Puerto Rico is one hour ahead in time than the eastern part of the United States. As he was preparing to leave the office for Roosevelt Roads the phone rang. He wondered who in the hell would be calling this early. He knew that his bureaucratic supervisors in Washington D. C. or Atlanta, Georgia, the regional office, would not be in their offices at 7:00 a.m. eastern standard time. He answered the phone and to his surprise the caller was John Hambrick the Assistant Chief for Investigations for the South East Region in Atlanta, Georgia. After saying hello, Menendez heard the recognizable voice of Hambrick. He said, "John it is kind of early for you to call, I hope it is good news, I have had enough bad news to last me awhile." John responded, "I will give you the good news first, you will return to the states as soon as you can, however you must be in Washington D. C. by August 5th or the day after tomorrow. President Johnson is going to make an announcement on August the 6th. We are having a large meeting of agents on this same day. I cannot tell you what it is about. We have made reservations for you at the Washington D. C. Hilton arriving sometime on August the 5th. Make your airline reservations immediately so that you will arrive as scheduled. Drop whatever you are doing and take care of this, you can resume whatever you are working on it a later date. The bad news is that you will be away from your home in Miami for several weeks or longer. Bring all of the clothing you need for an extended assignment." Menendez responded, "John, you are aware that because of the booming economy here in Puerto Rico since Castro took over Cuba, it is difficult at times to get a flight in such a short order. I may have to go first class if I can not get a regular fare." John responded, "Do what you have to but be in Washington on the 5th." Menendez continued, "Since I was only going to be in Puerto Rico a maximum of four days, I will have to stop in Miami, go home and get more clothing for an extended assignment." Hambrick answered, "Do what you have to but be in Washington on the 5th. By the way sorry that this has been so sudden, but you will understand when we have our meeting in the Ballroom of the Hilton Hotel at 9:00 A.M on the 6th. See you in Washington." Menendez responded, "Will do, good bye." The conversation was terminated.

Menendez knew the Hilton Hotel well; he had been there for other national conferences. Menendez immediately made a call to Roosevelt Roads. The phone was answered by a male voice. He was the duty officer of the day. Menendez explained to the officer that he had an appointment to speak to the station commander, Rear Admiral Andrew Taylor, but due to unforeseen circumstances he was not going to be able to make the appointment. Menendez then asked the officer to be connected with the Rear Admiral. After a brief wait, the Admiral answered. He and the Admiral exchanged pleasantries and then Menendez explained to the Admiral that he would not be there for his appointment and the reason. He also told the Admiral that he would return to Puerto Rico to speak with him but had no idea when this would take place. The Admiral understood and they hung up.

CHAPTER 2

Immediately after speaking to the Admiral, Menendez picked up the documents on his desk, stored them in the safe and proceeded to the airport. He decided to go to the airport personally. He was well aware the phone system in Puerto Rico at times would drop calls and besides it was difficult to conduct business via telephone. Puerto Rico was booming economically. The hotels were at almost 100 percent of capacity and travel between the mainland and the island was enormous. Prior to 1959, when Cuba was taken over by Fidel Castro, Puerto Rico could have been considered a third world country. After Castro, American tourists wanted to travel to the Island for sun, surf and gambling. Puerto Rico was the perfect place. It was a beautiful island, great beaches, a lot of history and gambling. Overnight Puerto Rico entered into the 20th Centaury. It was very difficult to find places to rent. Corporations that wanted to open offices in Puerto Rico were finding it difficult to provide the mainland employees they transferred to Puerto Rico places to rent. Services were very poor. There was a lack of skilled workers such as automobile mechanics, air condition repairmen, plumbers and any other skilled employees needed with the increased demand. This is why Special Agent Menendez decided to go to the airport personally to make his travel arrangement. He had learned that things could be done more quickly and accurately on a face to face basis.

The San Juan Airport was not really located in San Juan. It was located several miles east of San Juan in the community known at Isla Verde. The airport was very quaint. It was still sort of a third world airport. It was beautifully landscaped with tropical flora and palms. The airport was replete with their national tree called Flamboyan. In the United States it is called a Royal Poinciana tree. In Puerto Rico it blooms almost continuously and it is so full of red or orange blooms that you cannot see the green leaves. There was a small building but most of the business of the airport was conducted in the open with just a roof over the areas. The planes had to be boarded by walking on the tarmac to the plane and then using steps to enter the plane.

Because of the growth in the economy and the number of persons traveling, it was almost impossible to find a parking place in the airport complex. Menendez was lucky since he had an official car provided by GSA and could park in an area reserved for government vehicles.

He walked on one of the well landscaped walk ways to the counter of Eastern airlines, which had the most flights between Miami and Puerto Rico. He was very fortunate that there was one first class seat remaining on a flight to Miami the same evening. It left Puerto Rico at 5:30 p.m. Puerto Rico time and would arrive in Miami at 6:45 p.m. Eastern Standard Time. The flight was a little over two hours but because of the time difference; it made it appear as if the flight took a little over an hour. He made reservation and paid with a Government TR (Travel Request). The reservations were from San Juan to Miami, on August 4th and from Miami to Washington D. C. arriving in Washington at 3:30 p.m. on August 5. This would give him the opportunity to be with the family almost a day and to get sufficient clothing for an extended assignment

Menendez arrived in Miami as planned and since he was going to be gone for a few days he had parked his undercover government vehicle in the airport area which was reserved for federal government vehicles. He spent the rest of the evening and the next day enjoying time with his wife Cleo, and his two children. He packed enough clothing for three-week assignment. What wasn't clean was washed so that he could take it with him. He figured that if the assignment lasted more than three weeks, which it often did, he could use the hotel or motel washing and drying cleaning services if needed.

CHAPTER 3

Agent Menendez departed Miami for Washington D. C. on August 5th. After retrieving his luggage, he proceeded by taxi to the Hilton Hotel. The receptionist at the front desk confirmed that he had a reservation. Menendez provided his credit card to cover any charges that he might incur. The room was being paid directly by the U. S. Department of Justice, Civil Rights Division. The hotel was located at 1919 Connecticut Ave.

Menendez remained in the hotel working on some reports that were due for submission. He decided to remain at the hotel for dinner since the surrounding area of the hotel was not the best area of D. C. There was a lot of petty crime around the area as well a prostitutes trying to pickup guests of the hotel. He came across several friends and former co-workers and remained at the bar enjoying their company.

After having breakfast, Menendez entered the Ballroom where the meeting was scheduled to beginning at 9:00 a.m. By the time he arrived there were already a large number of the attendees seated or milling around reconnecting with friends. He found a couple of friends he had not seen in a while and sat next to them waiting for the meeting to begin. The ballroom was a cavernous room. It seats several thousand people however on this day there were no more than 500 persons in attendance. A large section of the hall had been roped of so that the attendees would sit closer to the stage.

At about ten minutes after nine, William Waldrop, the Deputy Director of the Office of Personnel Investigations, U. S. Civil Service Commission got on stage and called the meeting to order. After brief remarks he said, "The gentleman next to me is Larry Greenwood, an assistant Attorney General for the U. S. Department of Justice, Civil Rights Division. He will explain why all of you have been summoned to this meeting and the reason we have kept it so hushed up.

CHAPTER 4

Larry Greenwood rose from his chair and walked to the microphone. After welcoming everyone and speaking a few pleasantries, he began to speak, "Gentlemen as most of you know, Congress has passed the Civil Rights Voting Act. It will be known as the Voting Rights Act of 1965. This law will go into effect when President Johnson signs it into law before noon today in the Oval Office. It is the president's mandate, as well as that of the Attorney General Kattensbach, that the Voting Rights Act be implemented immediately upon his signature. There are several reasons for this, one being it is August and this November in most states there will be local, state and national elections including congressional elections. The law authorizes the Attorney General to appoint federal election examiner, election registrars and federal observers at polling precincts. This law was enacted in such a manner that only states that will be affected by the law are the southern states. The President wants to have examiners and registrars on site beginning today or at the latest tomorrow. This is to begin to ensure that all citizens, regardless of race, in the southern states will be able to cast their secret ballot in the forth coming elections. After this meeting, all of you will travel to your first destination and will be given credentials signed by the Attorney General authorizing each of you to ensure that all eligible voters are registered to vote, regardless of race or national origin, as long as they are otherwise eligible. This large group composed of agents and investigators from the different agencies is required because of the magnitude of the mission. We need this initial thrust in registering voters and later supervising the elections properly and expeditiously conducted. During your tenure as a registrar, examiner or observer, you will be assigned to the Atlanta Region of the U. S. Civil Service Commission. This assignment is only when you are actually performing in the enforcement of the Voting Rights Act.

While enforcing this law, you will not be carrying weapons; you will operate as civil law enforcement officers. The reason for this is because it is going to be difficult enough enforcing the law therefore, we do not want to give the appearance that we are gangbusters. We will do everything we can to solicit voluntary cooperation thus we should not be in a threatening posture. We will all act in a low key manner in an effort to solicit the support of the election official, community leaders and the population as a whole. This is why we also placed the responsibility of enforcement on the southern region of the Civil Service Commission. The commission has worked with southern states in many other areas. A large majority of the Commission employees are southerners themselves and this should also help in limiting opposition. They may not view us as carpet baggers or as if we were bunch of northerners trying to do them in." Greenwood rested and poured himself glass water. After taking a drink he asked if there were any questions thus far. None was asked.

Greenwood continued, "You may be wondering why we are so concerned in playing it low key, after all if it is the law and we can just go to the southern states and enforce it as gangbusters whether they like it or not. We may find extreme resistance and even wide spread violence. I need to give you a little of history so that you understand why the president is so determined that we do this with the least amount of animosity from the population of the states affected by our enforcement of this statue. All of you are college graduates with at least a B. S. degree since this was a requirement for all special agents or investigators. Most of you are attorneys or have other advanced degrees therefore you already know what I am going to say. I will repeat it so as to refresh you memory of American history. You recall the animosity and hate that developed during the Civil War. The southern states which were primarily democrats seceded from the Union over the slave question. The war began and President Lincoln and the Republican Party established the emancipation of the slaves. It was a bitter war, brother against brother, son against father and a complete hate between the Republican north and the Democratic south. By the beginning of Lincoln's second term, the end of the war favoring the north was eminent. In his second Inaugural Address to the nation President Lincoln spoke his famous phrase, "With malice toward none; with charity for all; with firmness in the right, as God gives us to see the right, let us strive on to finish the work we are in; to bind up the nation's wounds...." President Lincoln knew that in order for the nation to survive and live up to its promise, there had to be reconciliation. There would be no room after the hostilities to subjugate or castigate the south. He knew that the south had to be brought into the fold with honor and dignity. The worst thing that happened to the south was the assassination of President Lincoln. His death allowed all those Republicans and others to exercise their vindictiveness against the south, to subjugate them and make them pay dearly for the war. President Andrew Johnson attempted to pursue the ideals of Lincoln by attempting to provide charity for the south. This caused him to be impeached. Even though he was successful in the impeachment trial by winning by one vote, he was kept so occupied defending himself that he could not follow Lincoln's desire concerning the south. Immediately after the war the carpet baggers began arriving in the south. The term carpet baggers was coined because all the Republicans and northerners who were coming into the south to plunder it, had suit cases or bags as they were called. These bags were made of a carpet material and were woven on the outside just as a carpet.

These individuals with the consent of the federal government which was primarily Republican were determined to make the south pay for the war. They took over businesses, staffed city, county and state governments with officials who had not been elected. To add insult to injury, they brought many, now freed slaves, to run things. What the south was put through caused a deep imbedded hate for Republicans and anyone who was a northerner. For almost one hundred years, a Republican could not get elected in the south even as a dog catcher. This animosity helped create the Ku Klux Klan and other hate groups. Many Senators and other leaders of our country as late as the 80's had been part of these hate groups. U. S. supreme Justice Hugo Black had been a member of the KKK himself. It wasn't until the very late 30's through the 60's when Democrats began to prevail in the congress and presidency. When they began to attempt to establish civil rights legislation, the southern democrats left the Democratic Party and formed the Dixiecrats Party. Since third parties have never been successful in the country, many southern democrats became Republicans." Greenwood again stopped for a second and poured himself a glass of water, drank it and continued. He began again, "You all can see the convulsions the country went through and how long the hate lasted because the Republicans and northerners rode rough shod over the south. President Lynden Johnson wants to make sure that this does not occur again even if it is to a lesser degree. He knows that the majority of southerners realize that the south has to change its posture and allow blacks the rights that they justly deserve under our constitution. He is also aware that if this is done rough shod there will be a lot of opposition to the law and it will be more difficult to enforce.

Gentlemen, are there any questions as to why we want to enforce the law in a low key manner and not in a threatening way."? There were no questions. All of the attendees recalled their American history. They appreciated having been reminded of the problems that occurred after the civil war because of the way the Republican north handled establishing the peace. They realized that this legislation, the Voting Rights Law, could be volatile in enforcing since it goes against generational customs, the mores and the established social structure of the communities. These traditions and customs were unquestionably wrong and illegal but none the less, they existed. It was, therefore, imperative to do away with them by causing the least amount of resistance. Greenwood continued, "We have already prepared the assignment for each of you. You will work in pairs. In your assignment folder you have been provided with the necessary information as what your duties are and the name and telephone numbers of contact people if you need assistance or clarification. We have also provided the name and telephone number of an FBI agent nearest you who will be on alert to handle any emergency in which they have to intervene since you will not be armed and are serving in a civil capacity." The folders were passed to the attendees. Greenwood again began to speak after the folders had been passed around. He said, "You will notice at the bottom of the last page, you will find a name and the title Representative for the Southern Baptist Leadership Conference. These are individuals who are being sent to each locale by the conference. The mission assigned to them by the conference is to work with black community leaders, black churches and other groups so as to inform the black population that Federal Registrars are in the community and that they can go and register to vote. They have no official connection to you. They have been informed regarding the low key requirement of this assignment. They will do nothing to inflame the sensitivity of the citizens. As I have stated, they have no official capacity however, it would not hurt if you get to know these individuals since they may facilitate your work with the black community. These individual have been chosen for their integrity and level headedness. If you recall during the passage of the civil rights laws, the south was flooded with primarily young adults from colleges from all over the north. In their eagerness many conducted themselves in such a manner that inflamed the sensitivity of the population. Even southerners who were favorable to the civil rights laws became angry at the way many of these young people conducted themselves and the problems they created. It was reminiscent of the reconstruction days after the civil war. These volunteers who are going to be in the area will not create any unfavorable publicity or problems for you. Before you leave today please pick up your packet of forms that will be utilized in registering the voters under this law. Fill out one form for each person you register to vote. They will sign the bottom of the form which advises each of them that, the information provided by them must be the truth to the best of their knowledge. When you complete the registration process in your jurisdiction the completed forms which you will sign and authenticate must be taken to the local election officials and given to Clerk of the Court. You must advise the clerk that each and every name on these forms must appear in the eligible voters list in the next election regardless of whether it is for a local, state or national election.

You will conduct the registration at the local post office if there is room or a federal office building in the area. Your packet indicates in what location you will work at and that this facility has already been advised that you will be there and they will provide you space to do your job

After Greenwood finished speaking, Mr. Waldrop took over the microphone. He had monitors call out the names of the agents and they were given their assignment folder. The meeting was recessed for an hour to give the attendees the opportunity to read the instructions in the folder and ask questions as needed. This also gave them time to review the information about the community that they were going to as Federal Registrars and time to meet with the partner who would be accompanying each of them to the assigned community.

The meeting was reconvened. Waldrop asked for questions dealing with any topic regarding, location, duties, authority of the registrars or any other matter they needed to inquire about. After all questions were answered Mr. Waldrop made an announcement, "President Johnson has just signed the Voting Rights Act of 1965 and it is to be implemented immediately. As you noticed, each of you has all of your airline tickets and flight schedules in your folders. This conference is now over. Some of you will need to get to the airport in short order so that you can be at you assignment tomorrow. Call your contact person in Atlanta to tell them that you are in place and ready to begin your duties on the next day.

CHAPTER 5

Menendez's partner for the assignment was Jesse Thornton. Jesse was raised in Jackson, Mississippi but had been living in Atlanta, Georgia over twenty years. He attended Georgia Tech and then remained in Atlanta. He became a federal agent and had been assigned to the Atlanta Region from the beginning of his service. Agent Menendez knew Jesse. Even though they had never worked a case together, Jesse had conducted interviews on some of Menendez's cases when a witness was located in the Atlanta area. He had also met him many times at meetings and conferences. Menendez was pleased that Jesse was going to work with him. Being a Mississippi boy it would, hopefully, make it a lot easier to be accepted by the election and city officials as well as the population in general.

Their assignment was Demopolis, Alabama which is the largest city in Marengo County, Alabama. The airport that serviced Demopolis was Danielle Field, Montgomery, Alabama. Demopolis was approximately 85 miles from Montgomery. The flight time from Washington D. C. was a little over an hour to Montgomery. Jesse and Menendez boarded a flight out of Washington D. C. National airport at 2:00 p m. EST. They would arrive at Montgomery at approximately 2:30 p. m. CST. They were gaining an hour since Montgomery was on Central Standard Time. They arrived in Montgomery and went directly to a Best Western Motel where reservations had been made for them. It was policy of the department that the agents stay at a different city than where they were working at. This was a preventive measure so that some community hot heads did not know where they were staying. The road between Montgomery and Demopolis was a decent road. If they left their motel by 7 a.m. they would be at their post on time. They did not want to be there as soon as the offices opened. They wanted to give the election officials time to get organized for their days work.

CHAPTER 6

E ven though Demopolis was the largest city in Marengo County, it was still a very small community as cities go. It was very clean, the homes, streets and parks were well maintained. First sight of the city gave you the perceived idea of what an early American community would look like. The area never experienced any battles during the Civil War. The area is referred to as the Black Belt. This is has nothing to do with the black population but rather because of the rich black soil in the area. Most of the south has red or reddish soil. This area has very rich black soil.

After dinner Jesse and Menendez met in Menendez's room to discuss the plans for the next day. And to reacquaint themselves with the information in the folder that they had received and analyze the registration form that they had to fill out for each person who registered. As they sat talking about the plans there was a knock on the door.

Menendez opened the door and an African American man was standing there. He spoke and asked, "Are you Agent Menendez?" Menendez responded, "Yes, I am and may I ask who you are and how can I help you?" The man responded, "My name is D. J. Jackson, I work for the Southern Baptist Leadership Conference. I am the person who will work in the community where you will be registering black voters." Menendez asked D. J. to enter and as he did, he extended his hand for a handshake. Menendez closed the door. Jesse had already heard what D. J. had said. Jesse stood up and also shook D. J's hand and said, I am pleased to meet you." "Likewise", D. J. responded. After a few pleasantries D. J. began to explain what his role would be. He said to them, "As you were told, I am not here to interfere in the performance of your duties or to antagonize the local population. I will be working as stealthily as I can. My job is to let the black population and the black leaders know that you are in town and if they want to vote they can register with you. I will give them your location. At times, I will drive some of the folks to your office. I will be available to you if you need any assistance with the black community and black leaders. We are cognizant that if this program can be accomplished without antagonizing the local population the better the chance that there will be acceptance of it. We realize there will always be a few hot heads who will want to create problems. The way it stands now, I will be the person from the SCLU who will always be working with your team. This is so that we can develop a good working relationship and confidence in each other." Menendez and Jesse thanked D. J. and asked him to stay in the room while they discuss the next day's agenda. D. J. had already been advised that the team of Menendez and Jesse would be registering in the local post office. It was a small building but it did have an office with an outside door which would be perfect for the job. After completing their planning, Jesse and D. J. left the room. D. J. mentioned that he would be leaving the motel a lot earlier than they would. He indicated that he already had a couple of meetings scheduled with local black leaders.

CHAPTER 7

Jesse and Menendez arrived at the County Courthouse at about 9:30 a.m. They went to the office of the Director of Elections. A clerk behind the counter asked if she could help them. Menendez and Jesse displayed the new credentials that had been given to them. These credentials did not identify them as special agents but rather as Federal Voter Registrars. They asked to speak to Mr. Pruitt, director of elections. The clerk asked them to wait and in a few second she appeared with a man who appeared to be in his 50"s. He was stocky but not fat, had blue eyes and he had a head full of strawberry blond hair. He spoke with a heavy southern accent and said, "What can I help you with?" Menendez and Jesse introduced themselves by name and again displayed their credentials to him. They asked Mr. Pruitt if they could have a private conversation in his office. He agreed. He opened the swinging gate in the counter and they entered and followed Pruitt to his office which was located in the right rear of the main office.

They all entered the office, Mr. Pruitt sat behind his desk and Jesse and Menendez sat on two metal folding chairs. Menendez spoke, "Mr. Pruitt, we do not know if you are aware that President Johnson yesterday signed what is called the Voting Rights Act of 1965. The implementation of the law is immediate. Are you aware of this fact?" Pruitt answered, "I know that this SOB president has been working on a law to allow all of the "Niggras" in the country to vote. He is violating the constitution on the rights of states. Voting is a state matter. I heard he signed the law but am not familiar regarding what it says. I sure did not figure I was going to have fucking federal agents here in my office the next day. Why are you here?" Menendez and Jesse first told Mr. Pruitt that they were not federal agents but Federal Voting Registrars. Menendez proceeded by saying, we are not here to disrupt your operation. In fact you will not even know that we are in town. Under this law, we are going to register persons who desire to be on the voter rolls so they can vote in any and all future elections regardless whether it is a local, state or national election. We will register anyone who qualifies to vote under your state rules and regulations, regardless of race, gender or national origin. There will be no more poll taxes or examinations in exercising their right to vote. We will be conducting the registration process at the post office. We will be here several days. Once we have terminated our assignment, I will bring you the completed Federal Voters Registration form attested by us. You are required under this law to enter the names of these individuals in your voter rolls and provide them with a voter registration identification card. If any of these individuals names fails to appear on the voter rolls of your county it will result in legal action against you and your office. We will ask for and will receive an order from a Federal Judge allowing us to confiscate your election records from your office. I have just explained the procedures. I am confidant that you are a person who will follow the law even if you disagree with it." Mr. Pruitt responded, "I will do what is required of me and will follow the law however I am not going to proceed based on the bullshit you are telling me. I will follow whatever the county Attorney tells me are my duties." Menendez responded, "Fair enough. I agree with you. Your county or state attorney will be your advisor as to what you should and must do. I just explained the law to you. I was not attempting to give you a direct order as to what to do. I am sure that the county attorney will guide you in the right direction so that you can comply. This is a copy of the form that we will be utilizing when we register voters and when completed I will bring to you." Menendez handed Mr. Pruitt the form, he took it and threw on the desk as if he were not interested in what it said.

After Mr. Pruitt spent a few minutes ranting, complaining and cursing the President, Congress and anything else that came to his mind, Menendez and Jesse left the office.

After leaving the election office, Menendez and Jesse went to the post office to see the office where they would be working. The post office was small. It had the main customer area, a small room in the back where postmen could sort the mail in preparation for delivery. Most of the mail was for rural routes. There were to other offices. They entered the post office and asked the clerk if the postmaster was available. A lady in the back who was examining boxes heard the question and came forward. She stated, "I am Mrs. Griffin, I am the postmaster, may I help you?," Jesse and Menendez explained who they were. Mrs. Griffin responded that the office to her right was the office that they would use. She indicated that she really did not know what Jesse and Menendez would be doing but had been told that she had to provide a space. She stated that the space had been cleaned out and ready to be utilized by them. The pair explained to her what they would be doing while in the city. She did not say anything, however considering her smirk, it was evident she was not very supportive of blacks having the right to vote. She did not say anything because, she was a federal employee. Mrs. Griffin gave them two keys for the door that leads to the outside from the office. She said, "Due to postal regulations, you cannot have access to the post office operation area itself. I will keep that door between your office and our facility locked from the inside."

Menendez agreed that this was best since he did not want to have access to stamps, money orders or the mail. He also told her, "We will be working long hours and even when the post office has closed for the day."

CHAPTER 8

B y the time Menendez and Jesse had made their contact
with Mr. Pruitt and Mrs. Griffin and explained to them
what was going to take place, it was a little after noon.
They decided to have lunch. D. J. had stated that he was planning
to bring black citizens to register in the afternoon.

Jesse and Menendez knew that they could not or would not
go to have any food in local restaurants. They were cognizant that
once the community knew they were there to register blacks, some
food service personnel would spit on their food or who knows
what else. While having breakfast, they asked the motel restaurant
to prepare sandwiches, potato chips and a cold drink to eat for
lunch. They sat in the office eating their lunch and waiting for D.
J. to begin bringing in individuals who wanted to register to vote.
Just about the time they had finished their rushed lunch there was
a knock on the door and D. J. entered. He told them that he had
fifteen citizens that wanted to register to vote.

Menendez told D.J., "As you can see this office is not much
larger than a postage stamp. Bring two individuals in at a time and
the rest can wait outside until we can accommodate them." D. J.
stated "No problem we have vans and they can remain in them
till it is their turn to come in and register."

The first two individuals who came in were black males.
They appeared to be in their late Sixties. Jesse registered one

and Menendez the other one. Menendez noticed the fellow he was interviewing had very leathery hands as if he had worked with them most of his life in the sun. Menendez asked the man to sit and then pull out a Registration Form from his brief case. Menendez began the process. He asked for the full name and then also asked, "Are you here to register to vote in Marengo county?" The black gentleman began to speak, "I go by Henry Grant that is what I is called. I never had a birth certificate but I am called Henry Grant. My great grandmother was a slave and she told my mother that we got the name Grant from General Grant who freed the slaves in Georgia. He stated, "I don't really know why I is here, I was told to come and regis." Menendez told him, "You are here to register not regis. If you want to vote in this county on all election days you need to register. Do you want to register to vote?" Henry responded, "I recon I do. I've never voted before." Menendez responded, "We will take care of that," and began asking the required information such as home address, length of time residing in the county, date and place of birth. Any reason why he should not vote such as criminal records and so forth, and the party he was affiliated with. The form required that it be signed certifying that the information they had provided was the truth to the best of their ability.

What would have been a process that would take fifteen or twenty minutes took a much longer time. Henry was not sure of his date of birth. He thought he was born in Georgia and came to Alabama as an infant. His address was not a normal address. He stated that he lived all his life in the town at the first bend right after the railroad track as you leave town. A small house that was sort of green. He indicated that he had never been drunk and never arrested, that he worked the fields for some of the local white farmers. He also stated that he was told he was a democrat. When asked to sign the form, he stated that he did not read or write but that he always made his mark which was an X with a line through it. Menendez allowed him to make his mark. Since he would be certifying all of the registration forms and could attest to the fact that the mark was made by Henry Grant. All of the individuals, who D. J. brought to register to some degree or another, were similar to Henry Grant in not knowing much about their lives. Some were minimally literate since they had learned to write only their names.

Menendez and Jesse were appalled at what they had experienced. These poor individuals functioned socially at a level below most ten or twelve year old white children. The social system of the south had emasculated a majority of the black population of the county. Most were elderly which indicated that the younger black children left the area for a better life.

D. J. entered the office and told them that he was taking the people back to their homes and would see them at the motel. Jesse told him they would wait to have dinner with him.

CHAPTER 9

About an hour after arriving at their motel, D. J. arrived and came to Menendez's room to go out to dinner. Prior to D. J arriving, Menendez took advantage of the time by calling in the daily report which was required by the Justice Department Civil Rights Division. Depending on the size of the state and road conditions, the Justice Department set up monitoring offices. These offices were to be called if any problem arose, if the FBI, U. S. Marshalls or any other law enforcement agency needed to be sent to any location where there was or could be violence. Each Registrar had to make a verbal report at the end of each day to this office regarding the number of persons they registered, race and gender. The report also had to include information relative to the attitude of the local election officer and any other information that might be on interest. These local offices then sent a report to the State Department of Justice attorney who was monitoring the state. He in turn would submit the state report to the Attorney General of the United States, Mr. Kattensbach. By the time D. J. arrived, Menendez had completed his report and was ready to go to dinner.

They decided to eat at a Red Lobster restaurant which was located next to the motel. During dinner, they did not discuss anything having to do with the days experience fearing that someone might overhear their conversation.

After dinner, they returned to Menendez's room to discuss the day's events as well as to plan the next days' schedule.

D. J. stated, "By my count, we registered 62 voters today." Menendez answered, actually, there were 68. Six showed up by themselves. Menendez then asked, D. J, "How many more individuals do you think we will have registered by the end of the four days we will have been here?" D. J. responded, between those I will bring and those who may walk in, I would imagine we will have a total in excess to 250 registrants." Jesse stated, "I must admit that I was appalled at what I saw today. Having lived in the south all my life I know that the black population had not received their fair share of the educations funds and quality educators. The people who came to register to vote today were functional illiterate. They had a very difficult time with communication skills. A large number of the persons you brought to us did not even know what they were there for. You were some type of authority figure and they followed you not really knowing what they were there for. I felt angry at my self for having lived in the south all of my life and not realizing what our actions had done to this segment of our population. I will be honest when I was first told about this assignment I was not too happy, however after experiencing what I experienced today as to how these citizens were kept so ignorant, I am proud to be here. I believe that until the black population begins to elect blacks as well as other individuals, regardless of race who want to correct the system, thing will get worse for the black population. I feel a lot of pride that I am going to be part of this historical period of this country." Menendez concurred with Jesse and added, "To be honest, I knew it was bad but this also threw me for a loop. When I was growing up in Tampa, Florida during the 30's through the 50's Hispanics such as me were also objects of discrimination. We attended schools which student population was predominantly Hispanics. The discrimination was not overt but we knew and could sense it was there. Most Anglo parents would not allow their daughters or sons to date Hispanics. There were many public places where we were not able to go. Not so much because of laws but rather the non-Hispanic population, especially men and boys, would attack the Hispanics. Clearwater Beach in Pinellas County was a beautiful beach. They had a long pier for fishing, fast food stalls, and even dancing. There was a sign at the entrance of the pier which read "No niggers, dogs or Hispanics allowed". The saving grace in my case was that I had very light brown hair, green eyes and very a light complexion. As long as I did not give my name or speak with the Hispanic accent, I went every where. They saw me and thought I was an Anglo. The difference with the Hispanics and the black population was that we were white. Most of the Hispanics in Ybor City and West Tampa had a lineage from Spain even those who arrived from Cuba. Most Spaniards have very light skin, blond and in some cases even red hair. Only the Spaniards who came from southern Spain were of dark complexion because of the Moorish influence during the occupation of Spain by the Moors. Another advantage we had was that even though we lived in, what I now realize was, a Hispanic ghetto, we had a close knit family unit and extremely few children came from a single parent homes. We knew we would beat the system with education and we did. Today most of the doctors, lawyers, teachers, judges and other professions are Hispanics. This is why it is imperative that the black population of the south have the right to exercise their right to vote. Only then will they began to change the system in their favor. I am very proud of being part of this historical period in the United States"

D. J. stated, "This is the reason I am here instead of practicing law in some rich firm. I was very lucky to have had two parents who had college education and my father became a medical doctor. He was lucky to have been admitted to the George Mahary Medical School in Nashville, Tenn. which was primarily a black medical school. I feel that I have to give back to my people the opportunity that I received.

They decided that they had to be up early the next morning and D. J. and Jesse went to their rooms.

CHAPTER 10

The second day of registration was a lot more hectic than the first. D. J. was bringing six at a time and while we were processing them he left and would bring another six and take those who had completed the registration process back to their homes. Menendez and Jesse realized that they would be registering a lot more voters than the day before.

Outside of the post office things had picked up as well. All day groups assembled across the street yelling and cursing at each a new group of blacks who arrived to register. They would scream "nigger you may register but you are not going to vote." There were a few instances of rock throwing as well. Taking all things into consideration, the heckling was not as bad or intense as they had anticipated before they came to Demopolis to conduct the registration drive. This was not true in other locations in which, at times, there was a lot of violence.

During one of his trips ferrying voters to the post office to register D. J. came into the office and stated office, "You guys have it made in here. The crowd knows my car and they have been raising hell. They have thrown small boulders at me, thrown tack nails in my path, spit and generally have become very aggressive. They don't screw with you too much since they know if they do the U. S. Army or the F. B. I. will be here in no time. They know they can fuck with me all they want as I have no authority. Some of the population is refusing to get in my car and come to register. Having said this, it is not as bad as it could get. I am positive that when election time comes and they see blacks going to the polling places and actually able to vote," it is going to be a hot time in the old town. I hope I am wrong." D. J. gathered those who had registered and left to pick up another group. Menendez and Jesse could hear the crescendo of the noise when the crowd saw D. J. leaving.

Menendez and Jesse departed from the post office and before heading for the motel, they stopped at the elections office and provided them with the documentation of persons who had been registered that day so that they could be included in the official voter's rolls.

As they headed towards their motel in Montgomery Jesse, who was driving, told Menendez, "I have been observing a red pickup truck since we left the office. It appears to me that we are being followed. Some of these hot heads may want to find out where we are staying and my guess would be for a no good purpose." Menendez lowered his sun visor which had a make-up mirror. He adjusted it and was able to see towards the rear. He also noticed the truck. The truck never got close to their car but rather laid back often allowing one or two cars to be in front of them. This was done thinking that we would not notice the fact that we were being tailed. As agents, tailing cars was something that all agents have done in their careers in fact, it is a subject that is taught at the academy. The road was such that Jesse had no place to go. He had to continue on the road which made it easy for whoever was following them to do so. Menendez and Jesse decided to stop at a Holiday Inn motel which was located about 32 miles from Demopolis. They parked in a parking space in front of a room. They got out of the car with their brief cases as if this was where they were staying. They walked to the second floor and then towards the back. The pickup truck could not see them from the road or even the parking lot in what room they would have entered. Menendez and Jesse immediately came down another stair case and hid in the stair well. They heard the truck's engine making a circle around the motel and then leaving the parking lot and heading for Demopolis. They waited a good amount of time and then went into the motel's restaurant and had a cup of coffee. When they felt enough time had elapsed and the truck had not returned, they returned to their car and made the rest of the trip to the Best Western Motel in Montgomery.

While they waited for D. J. to arrive Menendez took care of all of the paperwork and reports he had to call in to the district office.

CHAPTER 11

D. J. arrived at the motel at about 9:00 p.m. He had called earlier from the home telephone of one of the black community leaders. He mentioned that he had gotten a tip that some individuals were going to follow him and run him off the road and God only knows what else they had in mind to do to him. He told Menendez and Jesse not to wait to have dinner with him. He stated that he was waiting till night fall and his friend would sneak him out of town. He was leaving his rental car at the friend's home. When he got to Menendez's room he told them that he was able to leave town without being seen. He asked Menendez if he could ride with them to Demopolis in the morning. Menendez responded, "Of course"

The three of them met at the motel's coffee shop for breakfast. As usual, Menendez went outside and placed a quarter into two different newspaper vending machines, the Montgomery Tribune and U. S. A. Today. The first thing that got his eyes was the headline, "A HUGE CROSS IS BURNED IN FRONT OF THE HOLIDAY INN". He went into the coffee shop and discretely showed Jesse and D. J. the news article about the burning cross. Jesse said, "Now we know why those mother fuckers were following us. They wanted to intimidate us and run us out of town. We sure fucked their plan. The stupid rednecks swallowed our ploy of getting them to believe that we were living at the Holiday Inn. They wasted a good cross."

Jesse, Menendez and D. J. got in the car and headed for Demopolis to continue registering black voters. When they arrived Menendez told Jesse to stop at the county election office. He wanted to keep these stupid bastards confused. They arrived at the office and Menendez said that he would go in alone. After a brief period he returned to the car, entered and they proceeded to the post office. D. J. and Jesse asked Menendez what he did at the election office. He said, "Well I talked to the deputy registrar and told him that he should tell the folks in town that just because they burned a cross in front of their motel did not mean that we would be leaving. I told him that we would not leave until we completed the assignment. I sort of feel sorry for the Holiday Inn; they will be having a lot of action and not even know what the hell is going on. The three of us should stop at the Holiday Inn on the way back. Get out of the car with our brief cases, hide as we did before, and grab a cup of coffee then continue our trip back to the Best Western."

They continued the routine of registering voters for the next two days. Surprisingly, there was less confrontations and intimidations from the local hot heads. It appeared that having burned the cross in front of the Holiday Inn was enough to let out steam and make their statement against the Government.

In the four days that the team was in Demopolis they exceeded their expectation by registering 340 individuals, almost all were blacks. D. J. knew the community and he stated if all of these folks vote, there would be enough votes to elect at least one black city council member. He also stated they could join forces with white politicians and even have more influence in the city as well as the county government.

Menendez added, "The monitoring of the election itself will have an important role to determine if what we have accomplished here will have any effect on the power structure."

CHAPTER 12

Chapters one through eleven were written in a manner so that the reader gets at least a flavor of how the Special Agents serving as Federal Election Registrars operated when going to the hundreds of counties all over the southern states to ensure that every citizen had the right and opportunity to register to vote in all elections whether they were local, state or national. It also provides a glimpse as to the reaction of some local citizens when they realized we were there to allow blacks to vote.

The president and congress knew that this Voting Rights law would have a profound and traumatic effect in the southern states and the southern communities. This law would be destroying local customs and a way of life that they had enjoyed for many years. The fact that these states and communities were wrongly denying constitutional rights to members of their communities, it was still very traumatic for them that some federal bureaucrat would be coming into their community to tell them how to run their elections. This also made them realize that the status quo of white dominance was coming to an end. They also came to the realization blacks would now be a political force in the community. The fear of the white citizens was the fact since, in many cases, blacks' outnumbered whites; they would be faced with the fact the community officials could very well be black citizens thus watering the power of the white structure.

Because of the aforementioned, the Attorney General and the Justice Department civil rights division instructed all of the agents (Federal Registrars) not to go into the community as GANG BUSTERS. We were required to follow existing local voter laws and procedures so long as they did not place any obstacle on any individual with the right to register and to vote whether they were white or black.

Because of this advisement we attempted to do our jobs professionally, respectfully and understanding the feelings of these citizens. In other words we were to avoid confrontations with the local officials or citizens.

Due to this requirement several times citizens as well as county officials and county judges engaged in a pattern of conduct that under other circumstances they would have been arrested. Cases in point; on one occasion a county judge who also was the county voter registrar became so angry, he did the unthinkable coming from a judge. When the Federal Registrar asked that the voting records be provided to him, the Judge became so angry that he pulled out a gun from his desk drawers and shot several times at the foot of the agent. Luckily he did not hit the agent and there was no indication that he wanted to kill him. He was extremely upset and lost it. Under normal circumstances this judge would have been arrested and brought to trial. Due to the policy of trying not to be too intrusive, nothing happened to the judge. Local officials who were present told the agent that the judge would be voted out of office for his actions. The judge was reelected several times after his actions. Because of our posture of working with the community in the manner we did, after a while there was less animosity towards us.

CHAPTER 13

Anyone who has travelled in small communities of any state and particularly in the south is cognizant of this fact. The communities, besides being small in terms of population, are very cohesive. Everyone knows each other either well or casually. Any stranger who comes to the community for any extended time, most citizens will be aware as to what the stranger is doing in the community.

When agents serving as Federal Registrars went to a rural community, the news that the Federal Registrars were in town was immediately spread among the community by word of mouth. Since we were viewed as the enemy; the individuals who came to destroy their social structure, presented many problems for us. The majority of citizens accepted the fact that we were doing our job and that they had no other alternative than to cooperate. There were many citizens who were very vocal in their confrontation with the Registrars. There was always a small group of individuals who felt they had to fight the federal government's action through violence, threats and in attempting to cause physical harm to the Registrars.

While working in the small communities, the Registrars had to be very aware of their surroundings. They had to determine if they were being followed and make sure no one knew where they were staying. More often than not, the Registrars traveled many miles away from the community where they were enrolling blacks and others to vote so as to find safe and suitable quarters. The Registrars where prohibited from carrying any weapons.

The Registrars had to be extremely careful as to where they ate. Eating in the local community restaurants exposed them of having their food spit on, exposed to urine or feces and even poison. While on detail conducting the registering of voters, many of us only ate canned or packaged food sold in grocery stores. We ate Saltine crackers or similar packaged products. We also ate Vienna sausage, canned tuna, canned fruits and other meats and vegetables that could not be tampered with. We could eat a regular meal in the evening when we returned to our motel which most of the time was many miles away and the management could be trusted.

I personally had several experiences which were not unique to me. I had a group of men in a red truck try to run me off the road over a mountainous road. On another occasion in a southern Mississippi community a group of "Red Necks" were threatening to hang me and my partner. On several occasions I had crosses burned in front of my motel room when the hot heads had been able to determine where we were staying.

CHAPTER 14

Before each election we went out to the local communities of the southern states to register the citizens, black or white. Since whites were never denied their rights to register the great majority, if not all, the individuals who registered were blacks.

During the registration period was the time when we had more of an opportunity to acquaint ourselves with the community and its dynamics.

Almost without exception the black community and the white community had established a way of life and a way of interacting with each other that was unique. Even though blacks were discriminated against in many ways, different water fountains, restrooms, sitting arrangements on the buses and so on there was still a modicum of respect. As a general rule many blacks had white friends who truly respected each other. Unlike large cities where blacks had been, and still are, relegated to ghettoes, the small southern communities, by enlarge were different. Blacks owned small parcels of land and more often than not, the next door neighbor's farm was owned by a white family. To some extent these rural farm communities were integrated as far as living in close proximity to each other.

By enlarge and particularly the business and political community had a paternal or maternal relationship with the black community. The white community felt that they treated the black community humanely and were willing to provide for their welfare when needed. Since these communities were so small, the people knew each other more often than not and treated each other with respect as long the blacks did not want to attend school with them, date their women or use those facilities which were designated for whites. It was not a rare occasion when a druggist or grocer provided a black family with free medicine or food.

The interaction that blacks and whites had developed living with each other was very confusing, sad and irrational to us, the registrars. Even though blacks were being denied basic constitutional rights and freedoms overtly, at least, I personally never became cognizant of any wide spread resentment towards the white population. I can attest to the fact that when the freedom groups began to come to the south from the northeast many of the older black citizens were angry because they felt these strangers were upsetting their way of life and the black/white relationships. Many in the black community felt that they were trouble makers. The freedom riders did not understand the relationship culture which had developed in the interaction between blacks and whites. They viewed the blacks, particularly the older blacks as submissive and called them "Uncle Toms".

These individuals came to the south with good intentions. However as we all know the road to hell is full of good intentions. They would go into a white restaurant and mixed couples would begin kissing, engage in improper conduct such as touching sexual organs and the like. Instead of helping us, the registrars who had a difficult time anyway, were making it more difficult for us by creating more animosity. They were enraging many members of the community who were normally cooperating with us to keep tempers and hot heads in line. If the so called freedom riders had stayed at home, it would have made it easier for us, the registrars, to do our job and for the communities to be more accepting.

CHAPTER 15

The second process required by the Voting Rights Act was that all elections in the southern states designated as enforcement areas had to be supervised by the Federal Registrars. These elections included local, state and federal elections. There was a lot of resentment in the south. Besides not liking outsiders coming in to run their elections, they were angry at President Lyndon Johnson because he gerrymandered the law so Texas, his home state, did not have to comply with it.

We never advised the local officials that we would be supervising their particular voting precinct. We would show up early before the polls opened and would advise them that we were there to supervise the election.

The law required us to supervise the election and to ensure their voting laws were applied equally to every voter. We could only interfere when there was a violation of their voting laws. If any voter was denied their ability to vote, we had the legal right to make a determination as to the legality of the voter voting. We were also required to go into the voting booth with the voter who declared themselves illiterate. The local laws allowed local officials to enter the booth with the voter, read the ballot to the voter and mark it in the manner in which the voter wanted to vote. When in the booth, we made sure that the voter was correctly read the ballot and marked in the manner they desired to vote. During the voting process we experienced as much or more threats than we had experienced during the registration process. More often than not, local officials as well as local police authorities participated in the intimidation.

There were times when the police would try to figure out a way as to arrest the Registrars or Observers. They would try through the use of traffic laws, speed limits and the like. We were always extremely cognizant of this.

There was a situation that occurred in a delta parish in Louisiana which provides an example of the authorities attempting to interfere. Our plan was after supervising the election, counted the votes and certified the results, we would drive back to New Orleans where we were staying. Prior to arriving in New Orleans the day before our preparations to supervise the election at this location, an informer contacted us. He told us that the county police, which was under the supervision of a county judge, who was like the dictator of the parish and a rabid segregationist, had a surprise for us. They planned to arrest us for a traffic infraction as we returned to New Orleans after the vote count. They were going to incarcerate us in a detention center that had no screens and the salt water delta mosquitoes would have eaten us alive. After they arrested us, they would figure what traffic law we violated. Having been made aware of this, we rented Dodge Chargers when we arrived at the airport. The Dodge Chargers were the fastest standard cars on the market at that time. We knew that the parish police were driving Olds 88's which were also fast but not as much as the charges. Needless to say, after the voting as we were on the only road that leads to New Orleans, the state police followed us and then turned on their lights for wanting us to stop. We hit the gas pedal and out raced them till we crossed the line on the New Orleans parish. They could not proceed. We stopped and gave them the middle finger.

CHAPTER 16

I firmly believe the Voters Right's Statue is the law which has done the most to provide blacks and other minorities undeterred accesses to the rights and liberties provided by the U. S. Constitution to all its citizens. The examples for this conclusion by me can be observed all over the country and in many areas of our southern communities. In a large number of southern communities and major cities black citizens have elected many black leaders to political positions, including Mayors, City Council members, Governorships, etc. Colleges all over the country and particularly in the south, have a good number of blacks in the student bodies as well as professors and college presidents. Great numbers of blacks and minorities have graduated from college with professional degrees in every field imaginable. Black and minority citizens who have availed themselves of their rights by taking advantage of opportunities provided them are doing well. These citizens no longer have to live in any particular area of the community. They now own fine homes in some of the better areas of the city.

The Voting Rights Statue has ensured that every black, minority or white citizen has the OPPORTUNITY provided under our Constitution to succeed and be the master of their life in securing the American Dream.

CHAPTER 17

I have described above all that the Voting Rights Act has provided blacks and minorities. By observing major cities or even small rural communities you can honestly say that I do not know what I am talking about. In city after city you see many primarily the black citizens living in ghettoes. Living in areas that are roach and rat infected. Areas where crime is rampant and children cannot go to a park for fear of being killed. A community in which unemployment is double that of the white community and where drugs are rampant.

My personal opinion as to why the black and minority communities are in the current situation is because of the black leadership. I will not mention names. Most of the black leader's names are well known. There are many who are not well known but are aspiring to become leaders. There are many national leaders attempting to the correct things however, the local level leaders have more influence because of their proximity to the citizens.

Why do I make this allegation? The leaders of any group must have those who he leads and/or attempts to control in a contiguous area. They must be concentrated in an area so that they can control their attitudes and more particularly how they vote. If the group they want to influence is spread all over town, it is not as easy to influence their voting. Some community leaders in these

black or minority communities go to the power structure of the
city, county or state and tell these leaders that they control such
and such a number of votes in this particular community. The
power structure in the community makes accommodations with
these so called black leaders. The accommodations can be money
for votes, appointed to political positions or political influence.
The political influence they can use for other activities they engage
to include but not limited to payoffs.

These leaders at times are the individuals who behind the scene
fight to maintain the status quo. They do not want these ghettoes
broken up because then they lose their political base and power
with which they influence politicians. There are documented cases
in which there was a move in the community to move blacks and
minorities away from the ghettoes for better living conditions.
These so called black leaders fought these actions because they
knew they would lose their political influence.

The Civil Rights Laws and the Voting Rights Law provided
minorities and blacks the dream Martin Luther King envisioned.
Some in these communities have or are in the process of achieving
these dreams but not for all. Many are still relegated to ghettoes
so these leaders can use the votes they control in the community
for personal gain.

The black communities suffer from inferior school, terrible
housing, tremendous unemployment, crime and drugs. If the
blacks would analyze their so called leaders and the political
individuals who claim to represent them they will discover the
following. Many are living extremely well. Many own very
expensive homes and other properties. Some do not even live in the
community. They sport expensive watches and jewelry. They have
good positions and respect among the local white leaders. They are
very vocal but do nothing that actually helps their communities.

A case in point: The black civil rights leadership has joined
other non-blacks organizations for the purpose of convincing the

black community that allowing illegal immigrations is beneficial to them. They take this posture because the great majority of these leaders are closely allied to the Democratic Party. The Democratic Party wants this immigration to continue because it is an established fact that when these illegal aliens have the right to vote, they will vote democrat. Many do at the present time by voting illegally.

If you are a black citizen try to convince yourself as to how this illegal immigration helps you. The preponderance of these individuals is un skilled. When they arrive in the United States, they of necessity seek employment. What jobs do they qualify for? What jobs can they perform illegally with a minimal risk of getting caught? They in fact compete for and undercut the salary black unemployed members of the community could be performing. The numbers of these aliens are such which they literally close the door of employment for our black citizens with little skill, out of the work place. I have had extensive experience in the labor market as a long time employee of the U. S. Department of Labor and as The Secretary of Labor for the State of Florida. In past years, black citizens with few skills could find decent paying jobs in the construction industry. They could find jobs in the different industries in which the business needed unskilled workers to work. Even in industries where there is mass production an unskilled person can be taught a task in a production line and receive very decent wage. Now you find that in the construction business illegal are being utilized because they work for less, they do not have to pay unemployment insurance, worker's compensation or social security for these employees. Therefore employers are benefiting tremendously by employing illegals. Many of these illegals are operating construction companies such as roofing, tile setting and others trades. These individuals often work on weekends. This is so as not to be caught by inspectors. This allows the owner of the property not have to get a construction permit. This saves the owner to permit cost as well as the property not being re-accessed for tax purposes. In years past black citizens could develop their own business such as handy man, lawn service, baby sitting and so forth. These jobs are more often than not being taken over by illegal aliens. There are hundreds of examples that I could quote which demonstrate that illegal aliens are not helping the black community. Yet, the Black civil rights leaders are selling this bill of goods to their population that illegal aliens benefits them. Many of your leaders have completely prostituted the Dream of Martin Luther King which was a dream for the black population who had suffered as a result of their ancestors having been abused financially and socially as a result of slavery. In his, "I have a dream Speech", he spoke of "little white children and little black children holding hands" not little black children and little alien children holding hands. He also spoke that his dream was that people would be judged by their character and not by the color of their skin. He did not say by their immigration status.

We who enforced the Voting Rights Law of 1965 did our job. I hope that the black population demands that their leaders do their jobs by first and foremost assuring they look after the interests of the Black communities.

I grew up in what I know realize was a Hispanic ghetto, Ybor City in Tampa, Florida. Our Hispanic community was concentrated in a few square miles. We also had "Our Leaders". They came by every election day for the votes. My father was earning $6.00 a week making Cuban cigars as were most of the community members. The money they were buying votes with, was at times more money than they earned in a week.

It took the Second World War for our citizens to wake up. The returning military men and women became aware of the problem. They were provided The GI Bill of Rights and became educated and bought homes away from Ybor City. It was like poking a big hole on a dam. You could not put the water back in. Today the children and grandchildren of the Hispanic community of the 20's and 30's are well represented in all areas of the professional community and in the power structure of the community. They do not have leaders who control them or have a ring on their nose to lead them.

The Voting Rights Act was intended as the instrument to poke a hole on the dam which was holding blacks and other minorities back from attaining their constitutional rights and the rights that the Declaration of Independence provides every citizen. It is very sad that for the most part a larger hole has not been able to be poked on the dam because the so called black leaders. They are the protectors of the integrity of the dam and they do not want any more holes. Leaders who have taken advantage of those that they profess to help have existed since the beginning of time, however in most instances those who have been subjugated by their leaders have been able to break the yoke. Blacks have not been able to totally do this even though many have.

Some of these historical leaders who have been able to control many members in their communities are among others listed:

Tammany Hall N Y, Frank Hague NJ, Ed Crump, Memphis, James Curley, Boston, Huey Long, La, Gene Tallmadge, Ga. Tom Prendergast, Kansas City, Richard Daley, Chicago and many others.

The hope, dreams and objectives of the Voting Rights Act of 1965 have not been fully fulfilled as intended and envisioned by Dr. Martin Luther King. Leaders have pacified their fellow citizens, with food stamps, telephones and other programs. Programs which congress has instituted to help the black community, at times they have been pilfered by the leaders themselves. Programs such as summer youth employment programs, HUD programs, food stamps and others. None of these programs have helped fulfill the dream. It takes good schools, decent housing, jobs and inculcating the citizens with the traditions of independence and not dependency and above all leaders who honestly and sincerely serve the community instead of themselves.

THIS IS WHY I CALL THIS SHORT STORY 'STOLEN DREAM'

OTHER BOOKS BY AUTHOR:

Violation of Trust

Abuse of Process

The Dancing Will Never End

The Answer

Stolen Dreams

Horror on the Sea Master

www.ingramcontent.com/pod-product-compliance
Lightning Source LLC
Chambersburg PA
CBHW030531290526
45786CB00004B/1685